CAMOUFLAGE

BEVERLIEY BRAUNE

CAMOUFLAGE

BLOODAXE BOOKS

ISBN: 1 85224 271 X

First published 1998 by
Bloodaxe Books Ltd,
P.O. Box 1SN,
Newcastle upon Tyne NE99 1SN.

Bloodaxe Books Ltd acknowledges
the financial assistance of Northern Arts.

Cover printing by J. Thomson Colour Printers Ltd, Glasgow.

Printed in Great Britain by
Cromwell Press Ltd, Trowbridge, Wiltshire.

For Thoran and Nova

Acknowledgements

The first five poems are reprinted from *Dream Diary* (Savacou, Mona, Jamaica, 1982) with minor revisions. Acknowledgements are due to the editors of the following publications in which some of the other poems first appeared: *Arts Review* (University of the West Indies, Mona), *Centre for Research into New Literatures in English (CRNLE) Reviews Journal* (Flinders University of South Australia), *Southerly* (University of Sydney), *Australian Women's Book Review* (Victoria University of Technology), *New Poets from Jamaica – an anthology: Savacou 14/15*, edited by Kamau Brathwaite (Savacou Publications, Mona, Jamaica, 1979), and *Water Wings: Poet's Union Inc. Anthology No.4*, edited by Phillip S. Nettleton (Poet's Union Inc., Sydney, 1996).

For me *Camouflage* stands as a significant signpost in a landscape of journeys. For travelling this far, I wish to thank Mervyn Morris, Kamau Brathwaite, Rhonda Cobham-Sander and Archie Markham. And I must thank the members of my family for their perseverance through my various adventures.

Contents

from
DREAM DIARY

below him still
another one is
turned away
from all that
self-abusing he

is looking down
to sea

MERVYN MORRIS
'A Drawing'
(for M.C. Escher)

A page from a dream diary

I have always been led to take long journeys:
or rather, pushed, like some stone
metamorphosed into brittle shale
on a cold-dry hillside
borne down a sheer valley
by a fatalistic wind.
If I must be that 'rock'
I'd rather be hornblende or feldspar
or some other non-precious stone
coloured in a futile greenness
that reminds me of mild,
drizzly summers – tearfully,
sensuously, snowless.
Or rather, I should say
(closer to my present state)
like this frost that must form
by the same force that
questions its very existence
into melting point
and later causes us
to long for it, frozen again;
the same force which
now icicles a half-tear, frozen
with snow-spoken strange things
as contrary as fire
or running water,
the undulant sea or
mist-hazed mountains or
God knows what.

I don't know
whether to stand firm
like the broken strand of hair
frozen on my forehead,
or succumb
like the growth of slime
in a pond of waterlilies
on the horny backs of waterbugs
and over the eyes of blotchy frogs

or…either way,
I'll be equal to the 12-hour bloom
that neither chooses to blossom
nor to fade.

In the outcome,
my only 'freedom' is
to acknowledge the chords
of life and death,
and what happens in between
– something that sounds like –
birds, twisted
deformed in mid-flight;
like the round multicoloured leaf
callipered, pulled
elongated to a tortured snap;
like the first-born,
short-lived, limbless,
a birth ungratefully twisted,
an abracadabra-mumbo-
jumbo mistake.
All around flounders
the idiosyncrasies of my blotted past
my fading present
and no more.
The wind-sounds take me back
always back.

I can never know
more than what I have known,
than what, at the time of its occurrence,
I added to the others
lengthening the list of incompleteness.
My only times of happiness
are those spaces after start
and before end of journeys, like this one,
when I am mercilessly alone
with the land, and I pause
at some unknown spot
where the snow drifts
in a frame-by-

frame motion
as in faulty
cinematography
or as in
a dream.

'Blue Bird, Blue Bird, in and out the window, Oh Mary, I am tired'

Have you ever walked
down some known
un-named street
with rows and rows
of tightly bulbed lights
and the encasements break
and let go, let free
some sweet, sensuous spirit
without scent or colour or sound,
just one divining touch?
Or have you ever walked
by some enchanted fountain
lit by one of those lights
and the spirit is set free
in the flight of water
reaching out to you,
like fingers of crystal droplets
sometimes tripping over the edge
of the fountain on to the stony pavement
in a kind of final self-sacrifice,
and you reach in,
become one of those diamond droplets?

And so you enter the cycle
of the fountain:
from the sucking whirlpool
up through the fierce jets
you are shot into the ignorant air
delicate and free.
You alone see yourself
and are soon saturated
with details of
passing through tunnels
windy lavender curtains
and sparkling people who
don't care who you are, or what you do,
or 'where you are going exactly?'
Like you, they care now

only for the watery music
of chattering leaves,
the whistle of flutes and yellow warblers
and tiny wind-chimes made of glass
ringing in your cool brain.

And then, a rustling wind channels you
into another world
where you meet ricocheting droplets
riding the arched columns of rainbows
all in a maddened laughter
dazzled with colours
of peafowls' backsides
fanlike, fluttering...
as in a combination
of roller-coaster-
ferris-wheel-merry-
go-round, all in one,
trapped with all the circus delights
and purple cotton candy...

And as suddenly as it came
the wind subsides,
leaving you now
to funny, saddened men
playing funny songs
at blue pianos,
accompanied by eighteen
powdered, smiling ladies
as if they are about to step on to some stage
as light as clouds...
and
as you watch and wait
you are thinking
just how full you are
that there's no need
for a heart or lungs or...
when

you hit the water

you are in the whirlpool again

with the others.

The fisherman's daughter dreams

She thought of standing naked on a rock.
She thought of the books
she had read,
the paintings
and pictures of paintings
she had seen.

And she went back
to the rock
and thought
how the wind was blowing
for miles
and miles over the sea
and how the moisture it carried
told tales
of soft feathers,
of the peopled dead,
of absence
and timelessness
touching the thin cool skin
of her naked body.

She felt the ocean rise
like a huge bosom
painted in bright colours.
It pulled her over
between the ocean swells.
It floated her
with the transparency
of imagined fish
and with a green
that pushed her under
and deeper into its waterflesh.

She thought how these imaginings
took her to the bottom
of a real ocean, and
how she sought to paint it,
to catch it, but
couldn't.

Dido

It was not a new world, but it was strange. She had not been there long, but she knew that in time they would find her.

Just a friend of the old woman, just an old house, just there to spend a short time.

On days like that day, it was difficult to tell the time. It passed away under sun-topped trees hurrying under to touch the dark wet soil. Sometimes it rolled off the leaves in sunlight, and at other times, it merged and was lost in all the dark green. Sometimes it seemed that the soil, the trees, the sun and the windless time were entrapped in a vision through that pane of glass. Sometimes she forgot that it was really framed in a simple white-painted sill with white window-strips, when her eyes crept back through the broken view into the darkness of the house. And her fingers let the heavy folds of drapery collapse, securely into place.

The way back to the room led her down a long corridor. Her fingers brushing satin armchairs with laced headrests. And then just tempting an image in the unused handfinished trays in their sullened brass and gold. Threaded ends of carpets creeping under voluptuous legs of mahogany. And as if fascinated by their exquisite form, attempted to lift the whole lot from the polished floor and disappear through the window to another world stranger than their own.

The sound of her stepping shoes between the ends of carpet gave an ominous chill to the large room and sent her on a trot as she passed the portrait of some old man in a worm-eaten frame. It seemed to be the thing most neglected in the house. There were always newly-cut flowers in the cracked blue vase. The metalware reeked of layers of polish, and there was never a trace of dust on the table or between the pine panels. It seemed that no one ever went close enough to the polished mirrors but to polish them, and then to make sure that no print of a finger or circle of breath was left to trace any human image.

All the long passageways led to other passageways, with inimical, empty junctions, as if there was no end to the old house. The longest passage led to a locked room, which for some reason she felt should have been open. And it had a most fascinating door knocker. Just a plain sphere from which hung the knocker itself clothed in tiny, careful leaves of gold.

It clung there as if it meant that door to have been the main entrance; or that the builders had made a deliberate mistake and that all the owners agreed not to say anything about it.

That was all she could think of. She felt it was such a good story. She felt she must have been the only one to have thought about it. Then she smiled and decided not to tell anyone about it. But she could not decide whether to touch it or just let it hang there. It was as if she expected it to start wildly knocking by itself. So she just let it hang there.

She approached the door to her room hesitantly, thinking to herself that someone was already in there waiting for her. She opened the door boldly and stepped in, indelibly surprised, to find only a brown lizard scratching furiously at the blinds to get to his freedom. She pretended that she didn't see it and just went over to the massive four-poster bed, receiving her maternally as she threw herself between the unmade sheets and pillows. Then when she could not hear the frightened toes of the lizard anymore, she lifted herself, crossed the room towards the blinds, pulled them up, and stood there looking through the window, waiting.

The room stood behind her, silent, unlit, except for rays of the setting sun fingering out the back of a decorated hairbrush where the tiny blue flowers faded towards the handle, a matching hand-mirror with the flowers still outstanding, and an empty musical jewelbox sitting on an old mahogany dressing-table. And then a small light hit the circular mirror and intensified into a beam that shot across the brown of her cheek and hinted at the tense throb at her temples.

For a few seconds, she was conscious of the tiny light playing under her eye, and decided to turn around to see where it was coming from. But suddenly in the half-turn, she changed her mind. And the beam soon shrank under the lengthening shadows. It flicked into her mind vaguely again when the dim headlamps of a car crawled into the driveway towards the front of the house. And she started out of the room.

The old woman had returned with her chauffeur, so it meant that the table was laid and that steaming trays were heaving a final breath in the stone oven. Everything not only happened on time here, but the appropriate things quite simultaneously. When all the lights went out, it meant that the old woman had found what Dido called 'the foreign peace of sleep'.

But Dido, she almost never slept. She always found something to do even it was just standing by her window from moon-up to sun-down. As usual, the old woman just passed her now as she came along one of those long corridors, with a bony brush of tired fingers and a smile that was lifted with all her heart but which she wouldn't or couldn't hold for long. The young woman didn't smile. She just watched the older until she was out of sight and then proceeded by herself to the front porch.

Sitting on the porch, she couldn't see very far with the thick growth of flowering shrubs near the house, and mango trees growing smaller and smaller as she strained and lifted her eyes. When her eyes fell closer again, she thought she saw something among the scantier limbs of the rose bushes. And then she was sure that she saw two people. She sat up taller in the old wicker chair.

She couldn't be sure whether they were men or women, but she was sure they could see her from where they were standing. And she shrank back into the chair because she knew they were also talking about her. She knew they had come for her now, standing there pretending, as if they couldn't be seen, dressed in such bright green, so close to the periphery of the light around the house. She thought of going in to the old woman's room and complaining to her. But she knew the old lady was always too tired to sympathise with anything. So she sat there watching until she couldn't see them anymore. She knew that it was because she was in the house that they didn't come in and take her away.

So, very confidently she got up and walked back inside. Thinking that if she went out again tomorrow at the same time, she would find them there again and that they would never be able to come in.

She traced her steps back through the large living room, through the smoking room, and the ladies' games room, smiling at herself in the mirrors. Smiling all the way until she came to the door with the gold knocker. She paused. Clutched a half-torn frill on her dress, and shuffled at the spot, at a disjunction.

For a moment she almost laughed out loud when she thought that all those who were after her were really locked up in this room. Then she stopped short and thought. How it could be the most beautiful room in the house. Her furious mind wielded imaginings of a series of small windows covering the east wall. She imagined waking up in that room. Seeing colours floating like air and falling on her and hiding under the bed-covers with her. Breezy branches throwing leaves into the glass and how they diffused through and fell in, on her face and breasts and arms and legs. More leaves were streaming in and more and more leaves smelling of pink and yellow pollen, and hairy insects. There were so many leaves. She had trouble breathing now. There were too many. She fought hard to push them off. To throw them back through the windows. She was grabbing, strangling those damned leaves, smashing them into splinters...when...she heard someone knocking, knocking.

And the leaves grew lighter and floated away. A trembling hand was glued to the knocker and when she recognised it, allowed it to let go. And the knocker fell on a final note, her thoughts subsiding again, like the wings of an alighted, frenzied bird.

She could hear her feet dragging on the old floor, leaving a trail of web-threads behind. She looked back for a moment and saw the drapery hanging defiantly over the large window in the living room. The drapes lay still like a solid sheet of rust that would soon disappear like dust under the light that fired the window at sunrise.

She was sure it was destined to happen that next day and so she decided not to disturb it at the risk that it might shatter before time, and that she would be the cause of it.

She walked more quickly now. The walls almost closing in. The corridor narrowing as she approached her room. She thought it was narrowing so quickly that she made one desperate dash to the door lest the walls should close in and cut her off completely. She always managed to make it in time.

A smile warmed at the corners of her mouth. She opened the door slowly and surely. And closed the door again.

When I want to be happy
(for Pat)

When I want
to be
happy

I
    imagine

rain fall
         -ing
music skip
         -ping
sun streaming in
through thin half-
closed eyelids,
breaths shifting scanty lashes
that play with dancing light
so that the corners of my eyes
curl in happy wrinkles
and blur the images
into rain so it falls
like soft down
like wraith-like cotton seeds
riding the wind.

I
    imagine

earlobes whetted
by the scent of sound
reverberating
within leaves in trees
and shrubs and weeds,
and as a sound licks round
the senses,
you are blessed
with the very weight
of a small bird
on a wisp of branch,

of screechy hanging bats, blind,
of the suffered snap
in the vulnerable veins of a leaf,
of the orange blossom, faded,
drooping from its weary stalk,
of the cry of lonely children,
of the dog locked out
of his familiar house,
of the expectancy in the creaking hinge,
of cold spectacles over watery eyes
of silence —

so you can only think
in juxtapositions of
hibiscus-red and gold-leaved-croton,
spray of pollen and smell of green mint,
something about...angels' feet shuffling
and children playing.

You see the sun going down,
the momentary blaze
of tops of trees
like water catching sunlight and holding on
a dance of music in every warm wave that flattens into perplexed
          ripples,
every moment lived into that subsiding sunset,
the sky-winds playing hide-and-seek with hummingbirds' wings
and you wish to throw yourself over to this captured dance

melt into all those airy colours
and crisp notes
and essences of pine trees
spindly-leaved and spread,
of soft-fleshed mangoes,
of uncombed hair
sliding and straying from
tight clasps of pins,
freeing themselves

into
    the
        soothing
                mood

of a
       drugged^{-up pop-}
jazz, that drags you
into its tempting lazy off-
beat, off-
           notes' side-
alleys' curly corners

and
   you
      follow

It was just the wind

I used to take
long roundabout walks
from school homewards,
burdened by a brown schoolbag
with its broken shoulderstrap
and a defective lock.
It would be at the height
of a warm, rain-threatened afternoon,
just fading out,
that time just before dusk
when it's coolest
and the winds are chaotic,
as the lighter afternoon stillness
is confronted by
the scattering ash
that feeds the evening,
and the drifting clouds
cover the sun,
so I could make the best
of my dark world.

With me, the evening,
the darker shapes and mock-tap-
mock of a music.
I would dream about
the unseen blossoms falling
in an unnatural slowness
to nestle in silvered webs
abandoned by red-legged spiders;
I would hear
the hushed whine
of an old dismembered tree
that drools after rain
in the hunger of aloneness;
And I knew that somewhere
there was a midnight
under which waves rippled
above floors clothed
by spawning fish,

salt-ridden shells,
restless winds in the veins
of transparent weeds.
I remember
that insomniatic cradle
called home,
where I spent every night
hypnotised by the ceiling
made of compressed board,
painted white to exhibit footprints
of untidy moths
and crawling colonies;
sculptural hollows
of dead spider-legs
and the dried-up jaws of insects
that shadowed
into the open dead mouths
of chattering men
with their baubled women,
who disappeared between the cracks
at any glint of light.

Yesterday I went walking again,
through flying pieces of rubbish.
They fell cackling on cement benches
all around me,
as the cement people stared
among the shadows and lights –
when those sunlit sharpnesses
between leaves fade,
when shadow and light
are married into
a hazy, dulled lightlessness
below the branches
of a banyan tree.

Today, my mouth tastes
of diluted air,
and I neither watch the clouds
nor know if
they still can
cover the sun.

Night after night
my thoughts clink
like half-melted ice
in this empty glass,
and even my cold feet
sense the tuned
estranging music
of a distant xylophone
that trips
in a foreign beat
and I am dancing
until the music stops,
sweating like a fevered child.

from
THE POINSETTIA FIELD

Call it reason overwrought
with the effort of balance –
pushed to the outlands of knowledge
with its mythopoeic ear unguarded
and its flanks assailed
by dream and desire...

RON PRETTY
'And Something Else'

No Fixed Addressee

Acuminate lines crease the reams unpacked,
separated leaf by leaf,
made to sit on each other
sheet by sheet,
padded, tapped firm on all four sides
so that I can see the size of the puzzle
I have set them today.
You see,
they want to re–
define me.

Woven words run together
unevenly
depending on how you look at them.
Sometimes they move backward
sometimes forward
and today they are shifting
sideways.

How far round the globe
shall I go to secure them?
Which latitude is best?
With whom shall I sleep?
How far shall I travel
to see where the lines will rest?
How often do I need to return
to see how weary they have worn?

It's time for lateral thinking.

Take the memory of my grandfather's eyes –
deep scorched ebony eyes
cooled by cataracts;
take the memory of my grandmother's eyes –
eyes clear as thin blue soup
doting upon her only son
even as he lies still and imperturbable
in the ground.

And how would they have me write these eyes?
That I see them only in one place?
That I see them with only one pen?
On a comfortably bound page?

For those who need to be comfortable
in a place that measures how far the pen must travel,
this is useful.
For when I hear them ask themselves
whose definition I should follow –
whether to lean this way or that on my journey,
it is necessary for me to stop
fix my visor
sweep the room clean of boundaries
with a smile or frown –
it doesn't matter –

it is not who will care;
it is that I am satisfied.

Yet I look around still
and ask: Who cares?
Needling lines,
these boundaries.

With stealth you can slip through
Anancy your way
over the boundary walls,
for the closer they veer
the more you see
that they are little precipices.

Step over the wall.
Glide down
No –
Fly down
on the fumes of your ink.
From here you can see new worlds
from back to front,
sideways;
you can see
the whole bloody comfortable compound
that you've left behind.

Aahh, isn't the gliding sweet.
Gives you time to think
laterally,
prepare for the landing
in another zone.

Consummate lines
criss-crossing
coursing the universe
receive me.
A fine laced pillow of surprises
greets my giddy head.
Pen and paper are waiting.

Here my voice is always new.
From here I see all boundaries a-new.
I can see their underbellies.
From here you can smell the fear –
write about it.
From here you can smell their expectations –
feel it.
From here you can dissect their requirements –
interpret it.
You must sing
and sculpt
and dance
and write this too.

So I shall take my mothers
where I wish,
with their flesh high on my nose,
wherever I find them;
I shall take lovers
to remember them stifling with life
wherever I find them:
in a cuttlefish in Sydney Harbour,
in a shark's upturned belly in Port Royal,
in the eyes of a Saxon warrior
guarding Wurzburgian rivers,
on the rocky hills
where banana plants creep down steep embankments
and, finding suppler soil,

take root against the wicked St Elizabeth wind,
on a old mahogany dresser
curved like a big-bellied woman
with wide brown arms
piled high with the dust of my memories
close and sleepy.

And I shall sleep when I want to
with those who love to glide sweet
laterally, into another zone,
listening to the wind
whistling sideways.

Mnemosyne Relentless

Rattle past ancient hamlets.
Re-plant the forests now.
Revisit places from that earlier time.
Look for a road,
a passage.
Make some sense of it.

The journey?
It began in earnest with groping litanies
the year before the coconuts began to die;
my backyard was an abattoir
of unclaimed carcasses.

Defining my price
or recalling the smell of blood-laden flesh –
the weight of the event
or the memory;
which is the more incalculable?

Mnemosyne came and went,
relentless,
discarded any questions.
Her function came as a revelation
when I was hardly looking:
I discovered that dreaming could transform,
could birth fabulous breathing monsters
from thin green blades.
I could see the earth miles down
to its seething centre,
from the gate of the fairies' magic boot;
fairies that protected me from the centre
from the manège of numbness –
the site where fear meets fear.

But the guards have dug in their taloned heels
keeping me to the formula of spells
beneath the door of the green boot –
griffin's grass.

How they carry me forward into life
with stranger creatures snapping at my heels
from the inaccessible plateau of my childhood,
the nightmares chasing me from island rocks
upon which my heart breaks, again,
where the earth still sinks in varying degrees
to meet the lost bones of men I shall never know,
where water runs purer than in any other place
so that people, with eyes in their wallets,
long polarised and paralysed,
seek the white liquid
for its purifying calcite memories of simple fishermen
gobbled up by fragile boats,
regurgitated upon uninhabited quays
where it is flatter, lonelier, sparser
and clearly the place for small fishermen.

Every morning
when the moon floats high
the fishers ride insubstantial boats
to meet head-on
the purpling blues,
to rival young marlin and small sharks
for the bounty of fish
they dream of.
        But
isn't that the Kraken
too far south?

Don't fall asleep yet!

Separate the studied from the learnt,
what is alive from what is nervy.

Forget fat fathers,
who know the proper place
for inconsequential fishermen,
carrying their wealth openly
as they alight with precious daughters
at the semi-circular drive in the school grounds,
beneath the Jesus looking down,
crucified from the north,

and Virgin Mary,
May queen mascot,
looking from the east.
There are many things to believe in –
the crucifixion,
the virgin birth,
the creed.

What cold sacrifice it is to find them again
as I am journeying in sundrenched corners
where intuitive discourses sift through the noises
of many old houses.
The voices creep up to me, unprepared,
bring with them the expectation
of another unsummoned engram:
the realities of remembering
reinforced by the sliding philo-
sophic over view:
first – this is how I remember it
then – this is how I see what has happened
and finally – this is how it could have been
as I see it now.

No one will ask me
from the plateau high beyond the cloud
'Do you believe it all –
the questions,
the voices?'

I must enquire
under my own steam
to find my mete-ing places

The First Place: Regret

Travelling alone:
passing landscapes
greeted the train again.
They flickered
upon her allergic eye.
She rubbed it to release the flint.
But the spark that waited there
launched her upon discordances,
branded her with crisp poinsettia leaves
falling from sun-dried pots
in the corner of the empty café.

The final conversation
was all that was left.

Yet she was relieved
to find that she could remember it,
the imagined life crueller
and crueller
each time it returned
turning upon her
like a cotton tree in flames.

The Second Place: Desire

Travelling separately:

They stood at the bridge for a long while, the silence between them inexorable. They looked at each other over the tops of Fishbone Water Fern that kept the stream in place beneath the bridge. Then they began wandering, zig-zagging across the moist dirt path leaving the brook with their watery images behind, locked in different vistas.

She saw herself entering a large hole – a drain that sucked from within her bowels; she could glimpse her own secrets. She pressed her ear to the wind with trees in it. It sounded like porcelain.

He was the captured one clinging to the zig and zag until they slowly drifted back to the landscape without, realised desire, the yearning to hunt out truths that had surfaced – an unconscious remedy for conscious inadequacies to unearth what may lie beneath untruths or the lie.

The Third Place: Loss

In the square beyond the bridge towards the dark house, mothers would stay out late into the early night to let the children play and to wait for the stranger who came to the woman at the window.

The women looked up at the skies and spoke over each other a little unlovingly about the lightest and swiftest snowfalls in memory. The children created new games as their mothers spoke late into the afternoon. Four girls and three boys caught pretend flakes from the sky to make a solitary imaginary snowman.

Few visitors passed them to traverse the bridge. And when the mothers were not looking, the children wandered to the edge of the silent water to throw in meagre mudballs and watch their drifting reflections mingle with that of the ancient stone warrior, his sword beleaguered by cracks for the procession of new workers migrating across the Nuremburg blackness.

The eager small eyes watched their squelchy offerings ride slowly, disappearing in full view, sliding: first as tenuous pithy bubbles upon the water's even movement, then as sinking islands of their fist prints. They were safe here while their mothers sold flowers, baked goods and bottled fruits. Safe until the big-bosomed sentinels folded their hats around their wide faces and swept them back with thick-girthed arms from the water's edge.

The women watched and waited for life to move too if only to a sluggish summer's flow like a seduction remarkable for what it might promise that other years had given. They spoke on as the children trailed behind; remarked on how they found it hard sometimes to remember an earlier kinder season. Some found it easier than others to report this, finding a word here or there to embellish the wishes between the hardness of the forgotten memory. Others were uneasy with the inability to forget while their senses fought in the air for familiar distant odours.

They lingered here as they often did at nights, near the post office, to see if the man smelling of spring trees would pass before they turned the corner. They shushed the children at every leaf fall, at every pebble that flew ahead of them on the path, listening for footfalls they had heard before. They would walk and stop and listen, turning at each pause; their coats, their women's bodies held close together like a medieval habit twisted in unison round them, carved them into mannequins manipulated this way and tilted that searching for the proper effect in a dresser's window. Some turned out of practice. One broad, harsh woman with black eyes slapped a boy's ear, called him stupid, and their dresses swirled around them straight again.

With the obscurity of a moment's passing they began to disappear – a pair here, three or four together there, one woman dropping back, trailing a good ten paces behind. The children, already losing interest in the spectre in the window on the dark hill across the river, rushed noisily past the dispersing female bundles. They dared each other to a race to the butcher's shop at the next corner.

But the woman, who had kept a little to herself, thought she heard footsteps out of pace with that which accompanies the insistent banter of children.

'I can see that woman in the window,' shouted a boy too tall and handsome for his years.

'Quiet!' said the boy's mother. 'Which window?' But she was already too close to the next corner and went on, leaving the woman who lagged behind.

The steps made themselves heard between the woman's measured pace. She looked back and saw him, feeling the satisfaction of warmth after the wait of longed-for intimacy. His lapels were buttoned tight, the deep collar of his coat shielding the back of his head. She let her eyes fall back in with the slowly receding shadows of the group ahead, like a blackmailer afraid to give away the identity of a clandestine benefactor. The stranger ascended quickly, his steps resounding with the urgency of someone who had miscalculated the time. He was half-way over the bridge. He was running. Then he disappeared into the hill beneath the dark houses.

The woman inhaled the air with private gratification. 'It's later than we thought,' she said to herself, counted her paces to the butcher's shop, then hurried to catch up with the others.

'I'm glad I don't have children's supper to worry about', she said to the mother of the tall boy.

And the night between the bridge and the corner turned with one woman; fell together into one neat blanket.

The Fourth Place: The Beest

I am the eighth blue wildebeest
hiding in a grassland herd,
my hindquarters like a horse's
my head, my humped shoulders
like a buffalo's
my beard, my mane
my long tail
my long curving horns
in–distinguish me
from the bulls.
I have become a brindled *gnu*
C. Taurinus

I skip too quickly for some
heavy with speed

to avoid the places
where swifter have fallen
while the herd
evenly spread
stands on its shoulders
in the wavering grass

The Fifth Place: Anger

I carry a red flag
in my right hand.
I am a woman
with a horn
to stab at a world
that stalks me with open wounds;
I shall cuckold it
watch it pulped
twist it through the crevices
of my left hand fitted with a fist.

I shall watch his blood run
through my fingers,
watch him masturbate
upon his grief,
know he'll die
upon some haggish rock.

The Sixth Place: Pity

Life is too short he thinks
and he looks down at the street before him;
he can glimpse
in the southern-most corner of his eyeball
the toes of his feet
feeling their familiar way

You smell today he thinks
as you did yesterday
and yes he knows
on the days before that

You smell of the filth
they want you to be

They need some body
to play the part
to dance the shuffle along the cement
left to chip and crack
to master the chink
where your toe fits

The Seventh Place: Acting

I am standing with a group of people near the bottom of a large stone stair (much like yours, but on the western side). I am outside a monumental building facing an immense statue or shrine. Behind that is a deep, thick wood with lofty, steady trees, dark into the horizon at their trunks, but there is some light hint of green at the tops of those near the building. We look up to the top of the stair and a priest-like figure, accompanying two or three new strangers, directs us to start the ceremony with holy songs. I open my mouth upon the lyrics like a magpie. But I will not remember these words when I awaken.

Later I am inside the building with dun expansive rooms and I look out onto a narrow doorway and see snowflakes falling lightly, sparsely. I say 'It's snowing' and rush to go outside (though I'm only a few paces away from the entrance of the doorway) to stand beneath the flow of cotton-ice. But by the time I reach the threshold, the fallen flakes have melted on the ground. The fall is thinning so I look up expecting more flakes but the fall has altogether stopped and I'm left thinking what it would be like to stand in falling snow. Then I seem to know that I'm there for a rendezvous or mission of some kind. There is a job to be done; there is something I'm supposed to do. I keep going in circles not finding the others who were standing on the steps with me outside. But I'm not worried because the house is so massive, vast enough to hide and hold us all at once.

Then I chance upon a young man, an old lover, maybe. I see him and miss him. Then we meet in a Cimmerian corner of one of the largest and deepest rooms. We touch foreheads and he says wistfully, crouching on top of a box or a piece of furniture just out of my reach, 'I miss you, but I'm all right' and he jumps down from the box and goes outside, but between us grows a thicker dark; I chase him. I become half-awake and pursue the dream, pursuing the young man, to kiss him, then I know I imagine I do and I feel everything the kiss is to reveal inside me, but it is like kissing a phantom. I can't touch him. My eyes are closed and he is smiling in my mind's eye. The smile of an observer. The way you smile into a mirror.

Wer aber sind sie, sag mir, die Fahrenden, diese ein wenig
Flüchtigern noch als wir selbst, die dringend von früh an
wringt ein wem – wem zuliebe
niemals zufriedener Wille?

But tell me, who are they, these travellers, even a little
more fleeting than we ourselves, – so urgently, ever since childhood,
wrung by an (oh, for the sake of whom?)
never-contented will?

RAINER MARIA RILKE
'The Fifth Elegy'
translated by J.B. Leishman
and Stephen Spender

Beyond: Bars

The summer sun
stripped shoots of grass
from the earth.
Sun heat rode the power lines
stretching through the jacaranda tree.
A child screamed
with harpies in her eyes.

It was as if the universe were flat
and all the suns raged down
multiplying upon their own refractions.

It was on one of those flat-earth nights
that Jimenez shaved her head
and
went out into the streets.

The Fig Tree

In the shadows of the fig tree
they are wrapped
like sprung tornados,
her thighs glistening with rapid light
that split the shade,
his head tilted back, way back
his arms taut with intention
his face firm,
the upsurge steadied

their cards fly out
into the black morning sky

King of Hearts with painted eyes,
he reveals himself to the lover
held high above the stage –
laughter
clatter
heel clatter

Fine hands like a boy's pace the air
trace her through
fix her beyond the veil
catch her as she would be

(Let your fingers slip
Say my name
Find a place to rest our memories
Let us discuss their rarity
see how they swing thus like fairy tales

I'll find the corner
where you're most comfortable
I don't know you there, rarefied, visiting
loving the neon lights
that dance off my lipstick
finding me irretrievable
while you sit waiting
quivering with music blasting in your ear)

Earth coloured carpet frets under his feet.
He wonders just where she has hidden her soul.

On Wednesday the show closed.
They threw champagne and claret over the balcony
at the seagulls.

(We watched them scatter white
a long, long way into the night)

Lunching with Friends

Before the men came to lunch
we loved each other a little
and knew it.

They ate with us and drank our Taltarni
under the monstrous fig tree
and the southerlies swept through us.

The early afternoon sun
hunted fig spaces
for our faces.

We laughed broadly.
We cried.

And when they left or we left them
I knew I had loved you
a little too much.

Good Mates

We shuffled – no,
you and my eyes –
seeking some private place
behind peacock feathers
(let us forget the man on my arm)
to exchange dreams
and would-be pat each other
across bristling shoulders
across heaving breasts
to take the stroking
far beyond what we should imagine

Light-footed and far from home
don't you wonder how to revive that space
between the orchids and the wandering yak
when you sat on your father's arm
knowing
and the curtains first lifted?

Why? Don't you want to reminisce now, friend?

Ma Donna

(for Donna)

She said: 'Mother,
why do you sit afore the fire,
breathing sherry and desire
when my dolls have gone a-wandering?
They won't know what to do
with their pointy breasts
and smooth clitoris
with their heads under their armpits
and fine painted lips
with silver bangles on their ankles.
Shall I go to find them
and will they bring me home again
with my pointed breasts
and smoothened clitoris?'

Busy for Sixty

at the end of the block
on the third floor
above the finely weeded roses
a plastic aloe vera needs dusting

plastic aloe doesn't know
what it means to wish to die
and succeed

He'd been in the garage a lot of late
re-polishing work benches hardly worked
shelving tomorrow's and the days-after jobs.

It may have taken six weeks to plan
six hours to tabulate in six columns...
that's part of the pre-obsession of being 59 –
to be busy for sixty.

Get used to the sound of it
without recalling in public
(tearfully and quietly)
Holland sun shine
in a boy's eyes.

Now memory is fact;
Fact, lost memory.

Loneliness glues the interstices.

A brand new Toyota
hallows success at 59
going on sixty.
Dust your reflection in the windshield
so that everyone knows
you were a good boy
you have no complaints
no comments
about the unbecoming of sixty.

Nirvana

A chant rose up.
He raised his hands.
The mob, ragged with waiting,
wept for nirvana.
'Please. Now!' it protested.

One edged herself
between him and heaven.

She pleaded:
'Please! And Now?'

The Night Bird

a granular chill-hung wind
rips leaves off the lap of Blackwattle Bay

the night bird whistles

her sumptuous black fare
discreetly masks Rilke's generous spaces

she speaks of morning-rites
when devils and our sweetest dreams
are sent warbling under her silvered tones

she makes us wish to lash ourselves
from blanched replies,
pitches louvres
beneath our pillows

Pelicans

Pelicans with clipped wings fan the sand
that bars an entrance to the bay,
their deep bills tasting flight upon crumbs
that graze the air.

A ferris-wheel dips with children circling
counter to pelican time.
A pedal boat frets new furrows
through the water's finest silt.

The flock sits waiting
for a shallow-breasted wave to crest.

Half a pond is missing

(or towards a better highway to the Kingsford-Smith Airport)

There was darkness
and the myriad beat ten thousand times
and there were more.
Then the darkness swelled
and greened in tendrils
with slow-motioned dance
to swan and duck feet
cleaned them
made feed
returning.

The darkness spread
thick.
Some called it wild;
some, unfit for children;
others, grounds to practise bread-
crumb-throwing from car windows.

So, when it happened,
duck and swan feet were light
with the familiar dark of moss, mud
eggshells.

They say it happened
while web-feet played a game of mud-crumbs,
when

three mornings
were taken for granted –
only three:

Half a pond went missing.

Private Concerto

The music soars through the cypress
cuts low to closely mown grass
lifts the odd fallen leaf from elm and beech
querulous with gums on the western side,
their leaves scrutinising the dry overlarge lawn,
bursting at their seams to shed old skin
to put on older skin –
discarded bleached barks falling:
the tones of a sombre cello
sidestep an intended allegro
for a finer space you may find
between reaches of harpsichord memory;
autumn wind
feeling true as a winter premonition
slows the tempo
hangs 'round the earth
sweeps you back
cello belly bound

Forgetfulness

A soft 's' slips off her tongue
reflects off old china dusted clean
than affection gleans

travels to unfamiliar territory
signals gone unnoticed
for too many years

meaning faltering
upon fear
finds language wanting

'libélula...alternado con paroxismos'
forgetfulness

the grammatically correct
stumbling upon the heart-felt

the mind clouded with too few details
unfolding and creasing
wrapping itself in clean-pressed tea towels

Just dessert

I should be happy tonight. Violent with its
vomiting the years that nurtured appetite
caviar, consommé, rancid cheese
each morsel carved hurriedly
inappetent

I expected the years to return
soon enough
infelicitously
inching their way
over each patent note tightly swallowed
with aromas high
and
perceptibly individual

but
these are foreign syllables
feeling their way to recognition
in odourless throes

I walked the streets
in search of inducements
that would send the wretch
upon another wave
and when I failed
came home again
drank red wine
urged the enharmonic knots
to find more lucid *vinculum*
to reveal themselves
with signatures of finer grain
but... nothing came

still clinging to the organ —
rash glory
greedy torpor
a disused promise —
acquittals fearing render
launched bitt'ric flavours
into the rigid meal
restrained themselves
upon familial bite
doubling
upon
fresh hunger

TV Snow
(*or* End of Transmission)

A desert plain
              heave in
pyramids
of
light

narrow steps of amber
prayer-ful palms
drought-fixed knees

       glass-packed grain
       of dubious shades

          prophets slip on terrazzo tiles

Falling Down

falling a-
part
narrow cones rise up
the air is cold with gas
flames blue
lightless
follow the white staircase
flame-topped spiral
smokeless

kiss one
blue
heatless
kiss and leave
the pilot's on

the chill sur-
rounds coning walls

see the child waiting lightless?

sense of noise
and falling down

Transformation

airy black-feathered tips
leaning
leaving
head first
shhh-
shaking
dust
soft-breathed
shh-
shaking the dryness
uprooting me
stiff with expectation
petal-lifted

the old form snaps